Reading Together

"No!"
said Joe

Read it together

This inventive story describes an everyday battle of wills between parent and child, with a happy ending! Here the parent uses imagination to persuade a reluctant child to go shopping. The book prompts lots of talk from parents and children about similar experiences.

> Do you like going shopping?

> No! I like the park.

> *"Now, what do you think of that?"* *"Yes," said Joe.*

Reading aloud is the best way to help your child get to know and enjoy a book. This book is particularly good to read out loud because of the rhyme and the voices of the parent and child.

The repetition of Joe's answer in the story helps children to join in quickly with reading the book.

> What does he say?

> *"Yes," said Joe.*

"*I know you want to play... There's lots to do to—*"

—day!"

By leaving spaces for children to join in, they will learn to recognize the pattern of the rhyme.

The words tell a scary story of witches, giants and ghosts, but the pictures make it all seem fun. Children can talk about their feelings towards these characters and the stories they're reminded of.

He's not a scary giant.

No, but are some giants scary?

The Jack and the Beanstalk giant!

Children enjoy talking about the story and the pictures. After reading the book, find a favourite picture and talk about it together.

He's small like Jack and there's a beanstalk.

And it says "Jack" in the giant's book.

For Joel and Holly

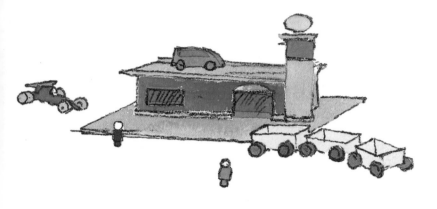

First published 1991 by Walker Books Ltd
87 Vauxhall Walk, London SE11 5HJ

This edition published 2001

4 6 8 10 9 7 5 3

© 1991 John Prater
Introductory and concluding notes © 2001 CLPE/LB Southwark

This book has been typeset in Times New Roman

Printed in China

British Library Cataloguing in Publication Data:
a catalogue record for this book is available from the British Library

ISBN 978-0-7445-6873-8

www.walkerbooks.co.uk

"No!"
said Joe

John Prater

WALKER BOOKS
AND SUBSIDIARIES

LONDON • BOSTON • SYDNEY • AUCKLAND

"Joe, fetch your coat, your gloves and hat,
Then find your other shoe,
We need to get some shopping done
And you are coming too."

"No," said Joe.

"Now don't be silly and make a fuss,
I know you want to play,
But we must get the shopping done,
There's lots to do today."

"No," said Joe.

"Oh, come on, Joe, you naughty boy,
If you behave this way,
I think we'll ask the Wicked Witch
To take you far away."

"Yes," said Joe.

"She'll make you eat disgusting things,
Like snake and spider stew,
Or slug and worm spaghetti –
Is that all right with you?"

"Yes," said Joe.

"And then she'll cast a dreadful spell:
You'll end up as a bat,
Or maybe as a slimy toad,
Now, what do you think of that?"

"Yes," said Joe.

"Perhaps she'll soon get tired of you
And stuff you in a sack,
Then give you to a passing giant
Who'll never bring you back."

"Yes," said Joe.

"He'll scoop you up and take you home
To scare you as he reads
All through the dark and fearsome night
Of dreadful giant deeds."

"Yes," said Joe.

"He might decide to have a treat
And grind you to a pulp,
Then cook you in a great big pie
To swallow in one gulp."

"Yes," said Joe.

"Or else perhaps he'll leave you
At a haunted house he knows,
Where floorboards creak, shutters squeak,
And no one ever goes."

"Yes," said Joe.

"The ghosts inside are wild and mad,
With glowing eyes that stare.
They hide in cupboards, walk through walls
And spook you everywhere."

"Yes," said Joe.

"They gather in a ghastly gang,
And swoop and wail and moan;
There isn't anyone alive
Who'll stay in there alone."

"Yes," said Joe.

"Well, really, Joe, you are so brave,
There's nothing more to say.
We'll just drive off and leave you here
All by yourself to play."

"NO!" said Joe.

"Oh, you know we didn't mean it,
We'd never, ever go.
Come and have a special hug,
A big hug just for Joe.
Now get your coat, your gloves and hat,
And there's the missing shoe,
We'll quickly get the shopping done
Then buy a treat for you."

"YES!" said Joe.

Read it again

Tell the story

Encourage your child to retell the story in their own words, using the pictures to help them.

He doesn't want to go shopping.

He wants to fly with the witch.

Is this her broom?

Yes, and this is her cat food.

witch

cat

Witch's shopping list

Children often know a lot about witches from stories told in books and films. They can draw or paint a picture of a witch and the things she has to buy when she goes shopping. With your help, children can have a go at labelling the witch's shopping list.

And then he stirs in two trees and a dinosaur.

Giant's pie

What goes into a giant's pie? Children can pretend they are giants and make a huge pie using a large, empty bowl and either modelling clay or a variety of toys as ingredients.

Ghosts
Using an old sheet or cloth, children can act out being a ghost in the story. What can ghosts do? How do they sound? Children can make up their own ghost story.

No!
Why does Joe say "No!" near the end of the story? Talk together about the ending and why he decides to go shopping after all.

Scary things
What is scary? You can talk together about what your child finds scary in books, on TV or in real life. Perhaps you could share some of your childhood fears.

Reading Together

Red Books 2-4 years

Yellow Books 3-5 years

Blue Books 4-6 years

Green Books 5-7 years